Salads

Step by Step Recipes of Plant-Based Salads: Detox, Lose Weight & Be Healthy.

MARIA SOBININA

BRILLIANTkitchenideas.com

Copyright © 2019 MARIA SOBININA
BRILLIANT kitchen ideas

All rights reserved.

ISBN: 9781091987548

DEDICATION

This book is dedicated to my beautiful family and friends, as well as to you, my reader. I am happy to share the amazing joy of preparing healthy meals with you.

MARIA XOXO

Table of Contents

Quinoa Tangerine Salad   4

Quinoa Roasted Sweet Potato Salad   8

Sweet Potato Asparagus Salad   12

Three Potatoes Salad   15

Quinoa Tropical Salad   18

Kirby Salad with Olives & Chives   21

Tropical Salad   23

Potato Kirby Salad   25

Simple Summer Salad   28

Merry Berry Salad   30

Tropical Fruit and Berries Salad   32

Quinoa Strawberry Salad   34

Morning Bliss Fruit Salad   37

Kiwi Strawberries Salad   39

Sweet Potato Salad with Olives & Chives   41

Roasted Cauliflower Salad   44

Quinoa Asparagus Salad   47

Cucumber Tomato Salad   51

Sweet Potato Mango Salad   53

Broccoli Cauliflower Salad   56

Roasted Eggplant Salad   59

Cucumber Avocado Salad   62

Tomato Basil Salad   64

Mushroom Avocado Salad   66

Cherry Tomato Salad   68

Quinoa Tangerine Salad

INGREDIENTS:

FOR THE SALAD:

1 Cup **Quinoa,** dry

½ Cup **Cranberries**, dried

½ Cup **Walnuts**, chopped

½ Cup **Carrots**, peeled, chopped

3 **Tangerines**, fresh, peeled

¼ **Onion**, white, chopped

¼ Cup **Cilantro**, fresh, chopped

4 **Garlic cloves**, peeled, minced

1 ½ Cup **Broth**, vegetable

¼ Cup **Coconut oil**, unrefined

1 Cup **Water**

Coconut oil cooking spray (to grease the pan)

FOR THE DRESSING:

1 Tablespoon **Vegetable oil**, unrefined

½ **Lemon**, juice of

½ teaspoon **Curry powder**, yellow

½ teaspoon **Cumin**, ground

½ teaspoon **Paprika**, ground

Black pepper, freshly ground, to taste

1 teaspoon **Salt,** Himalayan, pink

EQUIPMENT:

Medium saucepan, Large mixing bowl, Baking tray, Measuring cups, Kitchen knife, Vegetable peeler, Spatula, Food Processor & Shredding disks (optional)

DIRECTIONS:

MAKE THE SALAD:

Step 1: Rinse and drain quinoa. Preheat the oven to 365°F.

Step 2: Spray medium saucepan with a cooking spray, place it onto the stove and add drained quinoa. Lightly toast the quinoa to remove excess water. Stir periodically. This will take 3-4 minutes.

Add vegetable broth and salt, and bring it to boil. Once it starts boiling, reduce heat to low and let it simmer for about 15 minutes until quinoa becomes fluffy and broth is absorbed.

If there is not enough liquid, add water or vegetable broth. Once quinoa is ready, set it aside to cool.

Step 3: In a food processor equipped with a shredding disk attachment, shred carrots onto long stripes. (You can also use a vegetable peeler to shred the carrots)

Place shredded carrots onto a baking tray, chop onions and place them with carrots. Add minced garlic and mix it with the vegetables. Baste vegetables with coconut oil using a basting brush.

Place the baking tray into the oven and bake for 15 minutes. Once vegetables are ready, remove from the oven and set aside to cool.

Step 4: Separate tangerines into pieces. Cut each piece into 2 or 3 parts. Set aside. Chop cilantro and add to the tangerines, add dried cranberries, chopped walnuts, and cooled quinoa.

MAKE THE DRESSING:

Combine spices and salt in a cup and add it to the salad. Mix well. Sprinkle it with lemon juice and olive oil. Place into the fridge to cool for about an hour. Serve chilled.

Quinoa Tangerine Salad will keep for up to one day in a

fridge.

Quinoa Roasted Sweet Potato Salad

INGREDIENTS:

FOR THE SALAD:

1 Cup **Quinoa,** dry

1 Cup **Sweet potato**, fresh, cubed

½ Cup **Mango**, fresh, cubed

½ Cup **Pineapple**, fresh, cubed

1 **Avocado**, ripe, cubed

½ Cup **Walnuts**, chopped

¼ **Onion**, white, chopped

¼ Cup **Cilantro**, fresh, chopped

1 ½ Cup **Broth**, vegetable

1 Cup **Water**

½ teaspoon **Salt,** Himalayan, pink

Coconut oil cooking spray (to grease the tray)

FOR THE DRESSING:

½ Cup **Cashew nuts**, raw, unprocessed

3 Tablespoons **Water**

1 Tablespoon **Coconut oil**, unrefined

1 **Lemon**, juice of

½ teaspoon **Cumin**, ground

½ teaspoon **Paprika**, ground

Black pepper, freshly ground, to taste

½ teaspoon **Salt,** Himalayan, pink

EQUIPMENT:

Medium saucepan, Large mixing bowl, Baking tray, Measuring cups, Kitchen knife, Spatula, Food Processor

DIRECTIONS:

MAKE THE DRESSING:

In a food processor, combine cashews, lemon juice, coconut oil, water, and salt. Process until smooth. Set aside.

MAKE THE SALAD:

Step 1: Rinse and drain quinoa. Preheat the oven to 365°F.

Step 2: Spray medium saucepan with a cooking spray, place it onto the stove and add drained quinoa. Lightly toast the quinoa to remove excess water. Stir periodically. This will take 3-4 minutes.

Add vegetable broth and salt, and bring it to boil. Once it starts boiling, reduce heat to low and let it simmer for about 15 minutes until quinoa becomes fluffy and broth is absorbed.

If there is not enough liquid, add water or vegetable broth. Once quinoa is ready, set it aside to cool.

Step 3: Peel sweet potato. Cut on cubes. Place sweet potato on a greased baking tray. Baste with coconut oil using a basting brush and sprinkle with paprika and salt. Bake until it is almost ready.

Peel mango and pineapple, cut into cubes and add to the baking tray to the baked potato. Sprinkle with coconut oil.

Chop onions with a kitchen knife. Place on the baking tray. Add minced garlic and mix it with the fruits and vegetables. Baste vegetables with coconut oil using a basting brush. Once ready, set aside to cool.

Step 4: Cut avocado into cubes, place into a mixing bowl. Add cooled quinoa and cooled roasted fruits and vegetables, salt, spices, walnuts, and chopped cilantro.

Step 5: Pour dressing on the salad. Place in the fridge to cool for about an hour. *Serve chilled.*

Quinoa Roasted Sweet Potato Salad will keep for up to one day in a fridge.

Sweet Potato Asparagus Salad

INGREDIENTS:

FOR THE SALAD:

4 Cups **Sweet potatoes,** fresh

14 **Asparagus** spears, fresh

2 Cups **Carrots,** fresh

1 Cup *packed* **Baby spinach**, leaves

½ Cup **Pineapple**, fresh, cubed

½ Cup **Walnuts**, raw

¼ **Onion**, white, chopped

4 **Garlic cloves**, peeled, minced

Coconut oil cooking spray (to grease the pan)

FOR THE DRESSING:

1 Tablespoon **Olive oil**, unrefined

½ **Lemon**, juice of

½ teaspoon **Paprika**, ground

¼ teaspoon **Cinnamon**, ground

Black pepper, freshly ground, to taste

1 teaspoon **Salt,** Himalayan, pink

EQUIPMENT:

Baking tray, Large mixing bowl, Measuring cups, Kitchen knife, Spatula

DIRECTIONS:

MAKE THE SALAD:

Step 1: Preheat the oven to 365°F.

Rinse and peel sweet potatoes, dice into round pieces. Cut each piece into four parts. Dice carrots into round pieces.

Step 2: Chop the onion. Place diced sweet potato, carrots, and chopped onion onto a baking tray. Cut asparagus spears onto three parts each. Place onto a greased baking tray.

Step 3: Add minced garlic, paprika, and a pinch of salt and mix it with the vegetables. Baste vegetables with coconut oil using a basting brush. Bake for about 30 - 40 minutes, stirring every 10 minutes, until vegetables are soft and fragrant. Set aside to cool.

Step 4: Peel pineapple, cut into cubes and place into a mixing bowl. Chop onion. Add to the mixing bowl. Add arugula, chopped walnuts and cooled roasted vegetables.

MAKE THE DRESSING:

Combine spices and salt in a cup, add the mixture to the salad. Mix well. Sprinkle with lemon juice and olive oil. Place in the fridge to cool for about an hour. Serve chilled.

Sweet Potato Asparagus Salad will keep for up to one day in a fridge.

Three Potatoes Salad

INGREDIENTS:

FOR THE SALAD:

2 Cups **Sweet potatoes,** fresh

2 Cups **Potatoes,** white, fresh

2 Cups **Potatoes,** purple, fresh

2 Cups **Carrots,** fresh

1 Cup **Green peas,** fresh

1 Cup *packed* **Baby spinach**, leaves

½ Cup **Pine nuts**, raw

¼ **Onion**, white, chopped

4 **Garlic cloves**, peeled, minced

Coconut oil cooking spray (to grease the pan)

FOR THE DRESSING:

1 Tablespoon **Olive oil**, unrefined

1 Tablespoon **Balsamic vinegar**

½ **Lemon**, juice of

½ teaspoon **Paprika**, ground

Black pepper, freshly ground, to taste

1 teaspoon **Salt,** Himalayan, pink

EQUIPMENT:

Baking tray, Large mixing bowl, Measuring cups, Kitchen knife, Spatula

DIRECTIONS:

MAKE THE SALAD:

Step 1: Preheat the oven to 365°F.

Rinse and peel potatoes, sweet potatoes, and carrots. Dice onto round pieces.

Step 2: Chop onions with a kitchen knife. Place diced potatoes, purple potatoes, sweet potatoes, carrots, and chopped onion on a greased baking tray.

Step 3: Add minced garlic and pinch of salt and mix it with the vegetables. Baste vegetables with coconut oil using a basting brush. Bake for about 30 - 40 minutes, stirring every 10 minutes, until vegetables are soft and fragrant. Set aside to cool.

Step 4: In a mixing bowl, add baby spinach, pine nuts, green peas, and cooled roasted vegetables.

MAKE THE DRESSING:

Combine spices and salt in a cup. Add the mixture to the salad. Mix well. Sprinkle with lemon juice, balsamic vinegar, and olive oil. Place in the fridge to cool for about an hour. *Serve chilled.*

Three Potatoes Salad will keep for up to one day in a fridge.

Quinoa Tropical Salad

INGREDIENTS:

FOR THE SALAD:

1 Cup **Quinoa,** dry

½ Cup **Mango**, fresh, cubed

½ Cup **Pineapple**, fresh, cubed

½ Cup **Raisins**, golden, dried

½ Cup **Walnuts**, chopped

¼ **Onion**, white, chopped

¼ Cup **Cilantro**, fresh, chopped

1 ½ Cup **Broth**, vegetable

1 Cup **Water**

1 teaspoon **Salt,** Himalayan, pink

Coconut oil cooking spray (to grease the pan)

FOR THE DRESSING:

½ Cup **Mango**, fresh, cubed

½ Cup **Pineapple**, fresh, cubed

½ Cup **Cashew nuts**, raw, unprocessed

1 Tablespoon **Coconut oil**, unrefined

½ **Lemon**, juice of

½ teaspoon **Cumin**, ground

½ teaspoon **Paprika**, ground

Black pepper, freshly ground, to taste

1½ teaspoon **Salt,** Himalayan, pink

EQUIPMENT:

Medium saucepan, Large mixing bowl, Baking tray, Measuring cups, Kitchen knife, Spatula, Food Processor

DIRECTIONS:

MAKE THE DRESSING:

In a food processor, combine mango, pineapple, cashews, lemon juice, coconut oil, spices, and salt. Process until smooth. Set aside.

MAKE THE SALAD:

Step 1: Rinse and drain quinoa.

Step 2: Spray medium saucepan with a cooking spray, place it onto the stove and add drained quinoa. Lightly toast the quinoa to remove excess water. Stir periodically. This will take 3-4 minutes.

Add vegetable broth and salt, and bring it to boil. Once it starts boiling, reduce heat to low and let it simmer for about 15 minutes until quinoa becomes fluffy and broth is absorbed.

If there is not enough liquid, add water or vegetable broth. Once quinoa is ready, set it aside to cool.

Step 3: Peel mango and pineapple, cut into cubes and place into the mixing bowl. Chop cilantro and onion. Add to the mixing bowl. Add dried raisins, chopped walnuts and cooled quinoa.

Step 4: Pour dressing on the salad. Place in the fridge to cool for about an hour. *Serve chilled.*

Quinoa Tropical Salad will keep for up to one day in a fridge.

Kirby Salad with Olives & Chives

INGREDIENTS:

FOR THE SALAD:

3 cups **Kirby,** fresh

½ cup **Chives,** pickled

½ cup **Olives,** green, pickled

½ cup *packed* **Arugula**, leaves

½ cup *packed* **Baby spinach**, leaves

½ cup **Pine nuts**, raw

¼ **Onion**, white, chopped

FOR THE DRESSING:

2 tablespoons **Olive oil**, unrefined

2 tablespoons **Balsamic vinegar**

½ **Lemon**, juice of

Black pepper, freshly ground, to taste

½ teaspoon **Salt,** Himalayan, pink

EQUIPMENT:

Large mixing bowl; Measuring cups; Kitchen knife,

Spatula; Food Processor

DIRECTIONS:

MAKE THE SALAD:

Step 1: Rinse and towel dry Kirby. Dice onto wedge pieces and place in a mixing bowl. Chop onion, and add to the mixing bowl.

Step 2: Remove stones from olives, cut olives in half. Add to the mixing bowl along with chives, spinach, arugula.

MAKE THE DRESSING:

Combine spices and salt in a cup. Add the mixture to the salad. Mix well. Sprinkle with lemon juice, balsamic vinegar, and olive oil. Place in the fridge to cool for about an hour. *Serve chilled.*

Kirby Salad with Olives & Chives will keep for up to one day in a fridge.

Tropical Salad

INGREDIENTS:

FOR THE SALAD:

2 Cups **Cucumbers,** fresh

2 Cups **Pineapple,** fresh

½ Cup **Chives,** pickled

½ Cup **Olives,** black, pickled

½ Cup **Raisins,** brown, dried

½ Cup *packed* **Arugula**, leaves

½ Cup *packed* **Baby spinach**, leaves

½ Cup **Walnuts**, raw

¼ **Onion**, white, chopped

FOR THE DRESSING:

2 Tablespoons **Olive oil**, unrefined

2 Tablespoons **Balsamic vinegar**

½ **Lemon**, juice of

Black pepper, freshly ground, to taste

½ teaspoon **Salt,** Himalayan, pink

EQUIPMENT:

Large mixing bowl, Measuring cups, Kitchen knife, Spatula, Food Processor

DIRECTIONS:

MAKE THE SALAD:

Step 1: Rinse and peel cucumbers and pineapples. Dice cucumbers onto wedge pieces. Dice pineapples into cubes. Place in a mixing bowl. Chop onion, and add to the mixing bowl.

Step 2: Remove stones from olives, cut olives in half. Add to the mixing bowl along with chives, spinach, arugula, walnuts, and raisins.

MAKE THE DRESSING:

Combine spices and salt in a cup. Add the mixture to the salad. Mix well. Sprinkle with lemon juice, balsamic vinegar, and olive oil. Place in the fridge to cool for about an hour. *Serve chilled.*

Tropical Salad will keep for up to one day in a fridge.

Potato Kirby Salad

INGREDIENTS:

FOR THE SALAD:

3 Cups **Sweet potatoes,** fresh

3 Cups **Potatoes,** fresh

2 Cups **Carrots,** fresh

3 Cups **Kirby,** fresh

1 Cup *packed* **Baby spinach**, leaves

½ Cup **Pistachio nuts**, raw

¼ **Onion**, white, chopped

4 **Garlic cloves**, peeled, minced

Coconut oil cooking spray (to grease the tray)

FOR THE DRESSING:

1 Tablespoon **Olive oil**, unrefined

½ **Lemon**, juice of

½ teaspoon **Paprika**, ground

Black pepper, freshly ground, to taste

1 teaspoon **Salt,** Himalayan, pink

EQUIPMENT:

Baking tray, Large mixing bowl, Measuring cups, Kitchen knife, Spatula

DIRECTIONS:

MAKE THE SALAD:

Step 1: Preheat the oven to 365°F.

Rinse and peel carrots, potatoes, and sweet potatoes. Dice onto wedges.

Step 2: Chop onions with a kitchen knife. Place diced potatoes, sweet potatoes, carrots, and chopped onion on a greased baking tray.

Step 3: Add minced garlic and pinch of salt and mix it with the vegetables. Baste vegetables with coconut oil using a basting brush. Bake for about 30 - 40 minutes, stirring every 10 minutes, until vegetables are soft and fragrant. Set aside to cool.

Step 4: Chop Kirby into wedges. Place into a mixing bowl. Add baby spinach, pistachio nuts, and cooled roasted vegetables.

MAKE THE DRESSING:

Combine spices and salt in a cup, add it to the salad. Mix well. Sprinkle with lemon juice and olive oil.

Place in the fridge to cool for about an hour. Serve chilled.

Potato Kirby Salad will keep for up to one day in a fridge.

Simple Summer Salad

INGREDIENTS:

FOR THE SALAD:

2 Cups **Cucumbers,** fresh

2 Cups **Tomatoes,** fresh

½ Cup *packed* **Arugula**, leaves

½ Cup *packed* **Baby spinach**, leaves

½ Cup *packed* **Wedge salad**, chopped

¼ **Onion**, white, chopped

FOR THE DRESSING:

2 Tablespoons **Olive oil**, unrefined

½ **Lemon**, juice of

Black pepper, freshly ground, to taste

½ teaspoon **Salt,** Himalayan, pink

EQUIPMENT:

Large mixing bowl, Measuring cups, Kitchen knife, Spatula, Food Processor

DIRECTIONS:

MAKE THE SALAD:

Step 1: Rinse cucumbers and tomatoes. Peel cucumbers and dice into round pieces. Dice tomatoes into cubes. Place in a mixing bowl. Chop onion, and add to the mixing bowl.

Step 2: Add wedge salad, spinach, and arugula, to the mixing bowl.

MAKE THE DRESSING:

Combine spices and salt in a cup, add it to the salad. Mix well. Sprinkle with lemon juice and olive oil. Place in the fridge to cool for about an hour. Serve chilled.

Simple Summer Salad will keep for up to one day in a fridge.

Merry Berry Salad

INGREDIENTS:

FOR THE SALAD:

2 Cups **Strawberries**, fresh

1 Cup **Raspberries**, fresh

1 Cup **Blueberries**, fresh

½ Cup **Pine nuts**, raw

1 Cup **Pecans**, raw, chopped

1 Cup **Oats,** rolled

½ Cup *packed* **Baby spinach**, leaves

¼ Cup *packed* **Basil**, fresh, leaves

FOR THE DRESSING:

½ Cup **Strawberries,** fresh

½ Cup **Cashew nuts**, raw, unprocessed

1 Tablespoon **Coconut oil**, unrefined

½ **Lemon**, juice of

¼ teaspoon **Salt,** Himalayan, pink

1 teaspoon **Vanilla,** pure, extract *(optional)*

EQUIPMENT:

Large mixing bowl, Measuring cups, Kitchen knife, Spatula, Food Processor

DIRECTIONS:

MAKE THE DRESSING:

In a food processor, combine ½ cup strawberries, coconut oil, lemon juice, cashews, vanilla extract, and a pinch of Himalayan pink salt. Process until smooth. Set aside.

MAKE THE SALAD:

Step 1: Cut strawberries into bite sizes. In a mixing bowl, combine spinach, basil, strawberries, raspberries, blueberries, pine nuts, pecans, and rolled oats.

Step 2: Pour dressing on the salad. Place in the fridge to cool for about an hour. *Serve chilled.*

Merry Berry Salad will keep for up to one day in a fridge.

Tropical Fruit and Berries Salad

INGREDIENTS:

FOR THE SALAD:

1 Cup **Pineapples**, fresh, cubed

1 Cup **Mangos**, fresh, cubed

1 Cup **Tangerines,** fresh, halved

1 Cup **Strawberries**, fresh

1 Cup **Raspberries**, fresh

½ Cup **Pine nuts**, raw

1 Cup **Oats,** rolled

¼ Cup *packed* **Basil**, fresh, leaves

FOR THE DRESSING:

½ Cup **Raspberries,** fresh

½ Cup **Pineapples,** fresh

½ Cup **Cashew nuts**, raw, unprocessed

1 Tablespoon **Coconut oil**, unrefined

½ **Lemon**, juice of

¼ teaspoon **Salt,** Himalayan, pink

1 teaspoon **Vanilla,** pure, extract *(optional)*

EQUIPMENT:

Large mixing bowl, Measuring cups, Kitchen knife, Spatula, Food Processor

DIRECTIONS:

MAKE THE DRESSING:

In a food processor, combine raspberries, pineapples, coconut oil, lemon juice, cashews, vanilla extract, and a pinch of Himalayan pink salt. Process until smooth. Set aside.

MAKE THE SALAD:

Step 1: Cut strawberries into bite sizes. Cut pineapples and mangoes into cubes. Separate tangerines into pieces and cut them in halves. In a mixing bowl, combine spinach, pineapples, mangos, tangerines, strawberries, raspberries, pine nuts, and rolled oats.

Step 2: Pour dressing on the salad. Place in the fridge to cool for about an hour. *Serve chilled.*

Tropical Fruit & Berries Salad will keep for up to one day in a fridge.

Quinoa Strawberry Salad

INGREDIENTS:

FOR THE SALAD:

1 Cup **Quinoa,** dry

1 Cup **Strawberries**, fresh

½ Cup *packed* **Baby spinach**, leaves

½ Cup **Pine nuts**, raw

¼ **Onion**, white, chopped

1 ½ Cup **Broth**, vegetable

1 Cup **Water**

½ teaspoon **Salt,** Himalayan, pink

Coconut oil cooking spray (to grease the pan)

FOR THE DRESSING:

½ Cup **Strawberries,** fresh

½ Cup **Cashew nuts**, raw, unprocessed

1 Tablespoon **Coconut oil**, unrefined

½ **Lemon**, juice of

Black pepper, freshly ground, to taste

½ teaspoon **Salt,** Himalayan, pink

1 teaspoon **Vanilla,** pure, extract *(optional)*

EQUIPMENT:

Medium saucepan, Large mixing bowl, Large stockpot, Measuring cups, Kitchen knife, Spatula, Food Processor

DIRECTIONS:

MAKE THE DRESSING:

In a food processor, combine ½ cup strawberries, coconut oil, lemon juice, cashews, vanilla extract, and a pinch of Himalayan pink salt. Process until smooth. Set aside.

MAKE THE SALAD:

Step 1: Rinse and drain quinoa. Preheat the oven to 365°F.

Step 2: Spray medium saucepan with a cooking spray, place it onto the stove and add drained quinoa. Lightly toast the quinoa to remove excess water. Stir periodically. This will take 3-4 minutes.

Add vegetable broth and salt, and bring it to boil. Once it starts boiling, reduce heat to low and let it simmer for about 15 minutes until quinoa becomes fluffy and broth is absorbed.

If there is not enough liquid, add water or vegetable broth. Once quinoa is ready, set it aside to cool.

Step 3: Cut strawberries into pieces and place them into the mixing bowl. Chop onion, add to the mixing bowl. Add baby spinach, pine nuts, and cooled quinoa.

Step 4: Pour dressing on the salad. Place in the fridge to cool for about an hour. Serve chilled.

Quinoa Strawberry Salad will keep for up to one day in a fridge.

Morning Bliss Fruit Salad

INGREDIENTS:

FOR THE SALAD:

1 Cup **Strawberries**, fresh

1 Cup **Apples**, fresh, cubed

1 Cup **Pineapples**, fresh, cubed

1 Cup **Bananas**, fresh

1 Cup **Blueberries**, fresh

½ Cup **Pine nuts**, raw

1 Cup **Pecans**, raw, chopped

1 Cup **Oats,** rolled

FOR THE DRESSING:

½ Cup **Bananas,** fresh

½ Cup **Strawberries,** fresh

½ Cup **Cashew nuts**, raw, unprocessed

1 Tablespoon **Coconut oil**, unrefined

½ **Lemon**, juice of

¼ teaspoon **Salt,** Himalayan, pink

1 teaspoon **Vanilla,** pure, extract *(optional)*

EQUIPMENT:

Large mixing bowl, Measuring cups, Kitchen knife, Spatula, Food Processor

DIRECTIONS:

MAKE THE DRESSING:

In a food processor, combine bananas, strawberries, coconut oil, lemon juice, cashews, vanilla extract, and a pinch of Himalayan pink salt. Process until smooth. Set aside.

MAKE THE SALAD:

Step 1: Cut strawberries into bite sizes. Cut apples and pineapples onto cubes. Cut bananas into round pieces.

Step 2: In a mixing bowl, combine apples, pineapples, bananas, strawberries, blueberries, pine nuts, pecans, and rolled oats.

Step 3: Pour dressing on the salad. Place in the fridge to cool for about an hour. *Serve chilled.*

Morning Bliss Fruit Salad will keep for up to one day in a fridge.

Kiwi Strawberries Salad

INGREDIENTS:

FOR THE SALAD:

½ Cup **Strawberries**, fresh

½ Cup **Apples**, fresh, cubed

½ Cup **Kiwis**, fresh, cubed

½ Cup **Grapes**, fresh, halved

½ Cup **Bananas**, fresh

½ Cup **Orange**, fresh

¼ Cup **Raisins**, brown, dried

¼ Cup **Pine nuts**, raw

½ Cup **Pecans**, raw, chopped

FOR THE DRESSING:

2 Tablespoons **Honey**, raw

½ Cup **Orange juice**, raw

½ **Lemon**, juice of

1 teaspoon **Vanilla,** pure, extract *(optional)*

EQUIPMENT:

Large and small mixing bowl, Measuring cups, Kitchen knife, Spatula

DIRECTIONS:

MAKE THE DRESSING:

In a small bowl, whisk honey, orange juice, lemon juice, and vanilla extract. Set aside.

MAKE THE SALAD:

Step 1: Cut strawberries into bite sizes. Cut apples, kiwis, and pineapples onto cubes. Cut bananas into round pieces. Cut grapes into halves. Cut oranges into bite pieces.

Step 2: In a mixing bowl, combine apples, oranges, kiwis, pineapples, bananas, strawberries, pine nuts, and pecans.

Step 3: Pour dressing on the salad. Place in the fridge to cool for about an hour. Serve chilled.

Kiwi Strawberries Salad will keep for up to one day in a fridge.

Sweet Potato Salad with Olives & Chives

INGREDIENTS:

FOR THE SALAD:

4 Cups **Sweet potatoes,** fresh

¾ Cup **Mango**, fresh, cubed

½ Cup **Chives,** pickled

½ Cup **Olives,** black, pickled

½ Cup *packed* **Arugula**, leaves

½ Cup *packed* **Baby spinach**, leaves

½ Cup **Walnuts**, raw

¼ **Onion**, white, chopped

4 **Garlic cloves**, peeled, minced

Coconut oil cooking spray (to grease the pan)

FOR THE DRESSING:

1 Tablespoon **Olive oil**, unrefined

½ **Lemon**, juice of

1 teaspoon **Paprika**, ground

¼ teaspoon **Cinnamon**, ground

Black pepper, freshly ground, to taste

½ teaspoon **Salt,** Himalayan, pink

EQUIPMENT:

Baking tray, Large mixing bowl, Measuring cups, Kitchen knife, Spatula, Food Processor

DIRECTIONS:

MAKE THE SALAD:

Step 1: Preheat the oven to 365°F.

Rinse and peel sweet potatoes, dice it into round pieces. Cut each piece into four parts.

Step 2: Chop onion. Place diced sweet potato, and chopped onion on a greased baking tray. Add minced garlic and pinch of salt and mix it with the vegetables.

Baste vegetables with coconut oil using a basting brush. Bake for about 30 - 40 minutes, stirring every 10 minutes, until vegetables are soft and fragrant. Set aside to cool.

Step 3: Peel the mango and cut into cubes. Remove stones from olives, cut olives into halves. Place into the mixing bowl. Add arugula, spinach, chopped walnuts, chives, and cooled roasted vegetables.

MAKE THE DRESSING:

Combine spices and salt in a cup, add it to the salad. Mix well. Sprinkle with lemon juice and olive oil. Place in the fridge to cool for about an hour. Serve chilled.

Sweet Potato Salad with Olives & Chives will keep for up to one day in a fridge.

Roasted Cauliflower Salad

INGREDIENTS:

FOR THE SALAD:

4 Cups **Cauliflower,** fresh

2 Cups **Carrots,** fresh

1 Cup *packed* **Baby spinach**, leaves

½ Cup **Walnuts**, raw

½ Cup **Pineapple**, fresh, cubed

¼ **Onion**, white, chopped

4 **Garlic cloves**, peeled, minced

Coconut oil cooking spray (to grease the tray)

FOR THE DRESSING:

1 Tablespoon **Olive oil**, unrefined

½ **Lemon**, juice of

½ teaspoon **Paprika**, ground

¼ teaspoon **Cinnamon**, ground

Black pepper, freshly ground, to taste

½ teaspoon **Salt,** Himalayan, pink

EQUIPMENT:

Baking tray, Large mixing bowl, Measuring cups, Kitchen knife, Spatula

DIRECTIONS:

MAKE THE SALAD:

Step 1: Preheat the oven to 365°F.

Separate cauliflower into bite-size florets. Dice carrots into round pieces. Chop onion.

Step 2: Place cauliflower florets, carrots, and chopped onion onto a greased baking tray. Add minced garlic and pinch of salt and mix it with the vegetables.

Baste vegetables with coconut oil using a basting brush. Bake for about 30 - 40 minutes until vegetables are soft and fragrant. Set aside to cool.

Step 3: Peel and cut pineapple into cubes. In a mixing bowl, add spinach, pineapple, chopped walnuts, and cooled roasted vegetables.

MAKE THE DRESSING:

Combine spices and salt in a cup, add it to the salad. Mix well. Sprinkle with lemon juice and olive oil. Place in the fridge to cool for about an hour. Serve chilled.

Roasted Cauliflower Salad will keep for up to one day in a fridge.

Quinoa Asparagus Salad

INGREDIENTS:

FOR THE SALAD:

1 Cup **Quinoa,** dry

10 **Asparagus** spears, fresh

4 **Tangerines**, fresh, peeled

1 **Avocado**, ripe, cubed

1 Cup *packed* **Baby spinach**, leaves

½ Cup **Walnuts**, chopped

½ Cup **Cranberries**, dried

¼ **Onion**, white, chopped

¼ Cup **Cilantro**, fresh, chopped

2 **Garlic cloves**, peeled, minced

1 ½ Cup **Broth**, vegetable

1 Cup **Water**

¼ cup **Coconut oil**, unrefined

FOR THE DRESSING:

1 ½ Tablespoon **Vegetable oil**, unrefined *(or more to*

taste)

½ **Lemon**, juice of

½ teaspoon **Cumin**, ground

½ teaspoon **Paprika**, ground

Black pepper, freshly ground, to taste

1 teaspoon **Salt,** Himalayan, pink

Coconut oil cooking spray (to grease the tray)

EQUIPMENT:

Medium saucepan, Large mixing bowl, Baking tray, Measuring cups, Kitchen knife, Vegetable peeler, Spatula

DIRECTIONS:

MAKE THE SALAD:

Step 1: Rinse and drain quinoa. Preheat the oven to 365°F.

Step 2: Spray medium saucepan with a cooking spray, place it onto the stove and add drained quinoa. Lightly toast the quinoa to remove excess water. Stir periodically. This will take 3-4 minutes.

Add vegetable broth and salt, and bring it to boil. Once it starts boiling, reduce heat to low and let it simmer for about 15 minutes until quinoa becomes fluffy and broth is absorbed.

If there is not enough liquid, add water or vegetable broth. Once quinoa is ready, set it aside to cool.

Step 3: Cut asparagus spears onto three parts each and place onto a greased baking tray. Chop onions with a kitchen knife. Add minced garlic and mix it with the asparagus. Baste asparagus with coconut oil using a basting brush.

Place the baking tray into the oven and bake for 7-10 minutes. Once vegetables are ready, set aside to cool.

Step 4: Separate tangerines into pieces and cut each piece into 2 or 3 parts. Place into a mixing bowl. Peel avocado and cut on cubes. Add to the mixing bowl. Chop cilantro and onion, add to the bowl. Add dried cranberries, chopped walnuts, baby spinach, and cooled quinoa.

MAKE THE DRESSING:

Combine spices and salt in a cup, add it to the salad. Mix well. Sprinkle with lemon juice and olive oil. Place in the fridge to cool for about an hour. Serve chilled.

Quinoa Asparagus Salad will keep for up to one day in a fridge.

Cucumber Tomato Salad

INGREDIENTS:

FOR THE SALAD:

3 Cups **Cucumbers,** fresh

3 Cups **Tomatoes,** fresh

½ Cup *packed* **Arugula**, fresh, leaves

½ Cup *packed* **Baby spinach**, fresh, leaves

¼ Cup *packed* **Basil**, fresh, leaves

½ Cup **Pine nuts**, raw

¼ **Onion**, white, chopped

FOR THE DRESSING:

2 Tablespoons **Olive oil**, unrefined

2 Tablespoons **Balsamic vinegar**

½ **Lemon**, juice of

Black pepper, freshly ground, to taste

½ teaspoon **Salt,** Himalayan, pink

EQUIPMENT:

Large mixing bowl, Measuring cups, Kitchen knife,

Spatula

DIRECTIONS:

MAKE THE SALAD:

Step 1: Rinse and towel dry cucumbers and tomatoes. Dice onto wedge pieces. Place in a mixing bowl. Chop onion, and add to the mixing bowl.

Step 2: Add basil, spinach, arugula, and pine nuts to the mixing bowl.

MAKE THE DRESSING:

Combine spices and salt in a cup. Add the mixture to the salad. Mix well. Sprinkle with lemon juice, balsamic vinegar, and olive oil. Place in the fridge to cool for about an hour. *Serve chilled.*

Cucumber Tomato Salad will keep for up to one day in a fridge.

Sweet Potato Mango Salad

INGREDIENTS:

FOR THE SALAD:

4 Cups **Sweet potatoes,** fresh

2 Cups **Carrots,** fresh

¾ Cup **Mango**, fresh, cubed

½ Cup **Cranberries**, dried

1 Cup *packed* **Arugula**, leaves

½ Cup **Walnuts**, raw

¼ **Onion**, white, chopped

4 **Garlic cloves**, peeled, minced

Coconut oil cooking spray (to grease the pan)

FOR THE DRESSING:

1 Tablespoon **Olive oil**, unrefined

½ **Lemon**, juice of

½ teaspoon **Paprika**, ground

¼ teaspoon **Cinnamon**, ground

Black pepper, freshly ground, to taste

½ teaspoon **Salt,** Himalayan, pink

EQUIPMENT:

Baking tray, Large mixing bowl, Measuring cups Kitchen knife, Spatula

DIRECTIONS:

MAKE THE SALAD:

Step 1: Preheat the oven to 365°F.

Rinse and peel sweet potatoes and dice them into round pieces. Cut each piece on four parts. Dice carrots into round pieces.

Step 2: Chop onion. Place diced sweet potato, carrots, and chopped onion on a greased baking tray. Add minced garlic, paprika, and a pinch of salt and mix it with the vegetables.

Baste vegetables with coconut oil using a basting brush. Bake for about 30 - 40 minutes, stirring every 10 minutes, until vegetables are soft and fragrant. Set aside to cool.

Step 3: Peel the mango and cut it into cubes. Place mango cubes into the mixing bowl, add arugula, chopped walnuts, cranberries, and cooled roasted vegetables.

MAKE THE DRESSING:

Combine spices and salt in a cup, add it to the salad. Mix well. Sprinkle with lemon juice and olive oil. Place in the fridge to cool for about an hour. Serve chilled.

Sweet Potato Mango Salad will keep for up to one day in a fridge.

Broccoli Cauliflower Salad

INGREDIENTS:

FOR THE SALAD:

2 Cups **Cauliflower,** fresh

2 Cups **Broccoli,** fresh

2 Cups **Carrots,** fresh

8 **Asparagus** spears, fresh

1 Cup *packed* **Arugula**, leaves

½ Cup **Walnuts**, raw

½ Cup **Pineapple**, fresh, cubed

¼ **Onion**, white, chopped

4 **Garlic cloves**, peeled, minced

Coconut oil cooking spray (to grease the tray)

FOR THE DRESSING:

1 Tablespoon **Olive oil**, unrefined

½ **Lemon**, juice of

½ teaspoon **Paprika**, ground

¼ teaspoon **Cinnamon**, ground

Black pepper, freshly ground, to taste

½ teaspoon **Salt,** Himalayan, pink

EQUIPMENT:

Baking tray, Large mixing bowl, Measuring cups, Kitchen knife, Spatula

DIRECTIONS:

MAKE THE SALAD:

Step 1: Preheat the oven to 365°F.

Separate cauliflower and broccoli into bite-size florets. Dice carrots into round pieces. Chop onion. Cut asparagus spears into three parts.

Step 2: Place broccoli and cauliflower florets, carrots, asparagus, and chopped onion onto a greased baking tray. Sprinkle with minced garlic and salt.

Baste vegetables with coconut oil using a basting brush. Bake for about 30 - 40 minutes, stirring every 10 minutes, until vegetables are soft and fragrant. Set aside to cool.

Step 3: Peel and cut pineapple into cubes. In a mixing bowl, add arugula, pineapple, chopped walnuts, and cooled roasted vegetables.

MAKE THE DRESSING:

Combine spices and salt in a cup, add it to the salad. Mix well. Sprinkle with lemon juice and olive oil. Place in the fridge to cool for about an hour. Serve chilled.

Broccoli Cauliflower Salad will keep for up to one day in a fridge.

Roasted Eggplant Salad

INGREDIENTS:

FOR THE SALAD:

2 **Eggplants,** fresh

1 Cup **Mushrooms,** fresh

1 Cup **Prunes,** dried, pitted

¾ Cup **Walnuts,** raw

¼ Cup **Raisins,** brown, dried

¼ Cup **Cranberries,** dried

¼ **Onion,** white, chopped

4 **Garlic cloves,** peeled, minced

¾ cup **Goat cheese,** crumbled, divided *(optional, omit for plant-based version).*

Coconut oil cooking spray (to grease the tray)

FOR THE DRESSING:

1 Tablespoon **Olive oil,** unrefined *(more to taste)*

½ **Lemon,** juice of

½ teaspoon **Paprika,** ground

Black pepper, freshly ground, to taste

½ teaspoon **Salt,** Himalayan, pink

EQUIPMENT:

Baking tray, Large mixing bowl, Measuring cups, Kitchen knife, Spatula

DIRECTIONS:

MAKE THE SALAD:

Step 1: Preheat the oven to 365°F.

Cut eggplant into 2-inch wedge pieces. Chop onion. Cut mushrooms into large bite pieces.

Step 2: Place eggplant, mushrooms, and chopped onion onto a greased baking tray. Add minced garlic and pinch of salt and mix it with the vegetables. Baste vegetables with coconut oil using a basting brush. Bake for about 30 - 40 minutes, stirring every 10 minutes, until vegetables are soft and fragrant. Set aside to cool.

Step 3: Remove pits from prunes and cut them in half. In a mixing bowl, add raisins, cranberries, chopped walnuts, and cooled roasted vegetables.

MAKE THE DRESSING:

Combine spices and salt in a cup, add it to the salad. Mix well. Sprinkle with lemon juice and olive oil. Place in the fridge to cool for about an hour. Serve chilled.

Roasted Eggplant Salad will keep for up to one day in a fridge.

Cucumber Avocado Salad

INGREDIENTS:

FOR THE SALAD:

2 Cups **Cucumbers,** fresh

2 Cups **Tomatoes,** fresh

1 **Avocado**, pitted, cubed

½ Cup *packed* **Arugula**, fresh, leaves

½ Cup *packed* **Baby spinach**, fresh, leaves

¼ Cup *packed* **Basil**, fresh, leaves

¼ **Onion**, white, chopped

FOR THE DRESSING:

2 Tablespoons **Olive oil**, unrefined

1 Tablespoons **Balsamic vinegar**

½ **Lemon**, juice of

Black pepper, freshly ground, to taste

1 teaspoon **Salt,** Himalayan, pink

EQUIPMENT:

Large mixing bowl, Measuring cups, Kitchen knife,

Spatula

DIRECTIONS:

MAKE THE SALAD:

Step 1: Rinse and towel dry cucumbers and tomatoes, dice them into wedge pieces and place into a mixing bowl. Cut avocado in half and remove the pit. Cut it in cubes. Chop onion, and add to the mixing bowl.

Step 2: Add basil, spinach, arugula, and pine nuts to the mixing bowl.

MAKE THE DRESSING:

Combine spices and salt in a cup, add it to the salad. Mix well. Sprinkle with lemon juice and olive oil. Place in the fridge to cool for about an hour. Serve chilled.

Cucumber Avocado Salad will keep for up to one day in a fridge.

Tomato Basil Salad

INGREDIENTS:

FOR THE SALAD:

1 Cup **Cucumbers,** fresh

4 Cups **Tomatoes,** fresh

¼ Cup *packed* **Arugula**, fresh, leaves

¼ Cup *packed* **Basil**, fresh, leaves

½ **Onion**, white, chopped

FOR THE DRESSING:

1 Tablespoons **Olive oil**, unrefined *(more to taste)*

2 Tablespoons **Balsamic vinegar**

½ **Lemon**, juice of

Black pepper, freshly ground, to taste

1 teaspoon **Salt,** Himalayan, pink

EQUIPMENT:

Large mixing bowl, Measuring cups, Kitchen knife, Spatula

DIRECTIONS:

MAKE THE SALAD:

Step 1: Rinse and towel dry cucumbers and tomatoes, dice them into wedge pieces and place into a mixing bowl. Chop onion, and add to the mixing bowl.

Step 2: Add basil, spinach, arugula, and pine nuts to the mixing bowl.

MAKE THE DRESSING:

Combine spices and salt in a cup, add it to the salad. Mix well. Sprinkle with lemon juice and olive oil. Place in the fridge to cool for about an hour. Serve chilled.

Tomato Basil Salad will keep for up to one day in a fridge.

Mushroom Avocado Salad

INGREDIENTS:

FOR THE SALAD:

3 Cups **Mushrooms,** white, fresh

1 **Avocado,** pitted, cubed

1 head **Romaine lettuce**, chopped

½ Cup *packed* **Baby spinach**, fresh, leaves

¼ **Onion**, white, chopped

FOR THE DRESSING:

2 Tablespoons **Olive oil**, unrefined

1 Tablespoon **Balsamic vinegar**

½ **Lemon**, juice of

Black pepper, freshly ground, to taste

½ teaspoon **Salt**, Himalayan, pink

EQUIPMENT:

Large mixing bowl, Measuring cups, Kitchen knife, Spatula

DIRECTIONS:

MAKE THE SALAD:

Step 1: Chop romaine lettuce into 2-inch wedge pieces and place in a mixing bowl. Chop onion and add to the mixing bowl.

Step 2: Remove pit from the avocado and cut avocados into cubes. Slice mushrooms into thin slices and add to the mixing bowl. Add baby spinach.

MAKE THE DRESSING:

Combine spices and salt in a cup, add it to the salad. Mix well. Sprinkle with lemon juice and olive oil. Place in the fridge to cool for about an hour. Serve chilled.

Mushroom Avocado Salad will keep for up to one day in a fridge.

Cherry Tomato Salad

INGREDIENTS:

FOR THE SALAD:

4 Cups **Cherry tomatoes,** fresh, halved

2 Cups **Cucumbers,** fresh

1 **Avocado,** pitted, cubed

¼ Cup *packed* **Arugula**, fresh, leaves

¼ Cup *packed* **Basil**, fresh, leaves

2 cloves **Garlic**, peeled, chopped

½ **Onion**, white, chopped

FOR THE DRESSING:

2 Tablespoons **Olive oil**, unrefined *(more to taste)*

½ Tablespoon **Balsamic vinegar**

½ **Lemon**, juice of

Black pepper, freshly ground, to taste

1 teaspoon **Salt,** Himalayan, pink

EQUIPMENT:

Large mixing bowl, Measuring cups, Kitchen knife,

Spatula

DIRECTIONS:

MAKE THE SALAD:

Step 1: Rinse and towel dry cucumbers and tomatoes. Dice cucumbers into wedge pieces and place them into a mixing bowl. Cut cherry tomatoes in half. Chop onion and add to the mixing bowl. Remove pit from the avocado and cut it into cubes.

Step 2: Add basil, and arugula to the mixing bowl.

MAKE THE DRESSING:

Combine spices and salt in a cup, add it to the salad. Mix well. Sprinkle with lemon juice and olive oil. Place in the fridge to cool for about an hour. Serve chilled.

Cherry Tomato Salad will keep for up to one day in a fridge.

Thank You for Purchasing This Book!

I create and test recipes for you. I hope you enjoyed these recipes.

Your review of this book helps me succeed & grow. If you enjoyed this book, please leave me a short (1-2 sentence) review on Amazon.

Thank you so much for reviewing this book!

Do you have any questions?
Email me at: **Maria@BRILLIANTkithenideas.com**

MARIA SOBININA
BRILLIANT kitchen ideas

Would you like to learn cooking techniques and tips? Visit us at:

www. BRILLIANTkitchenideas.com

Printed in Great Britain
by Amazon